P9-CRJ-897

A Day in the Deep

by Kevin Kurtz

illustrated by Erin E. Hunter

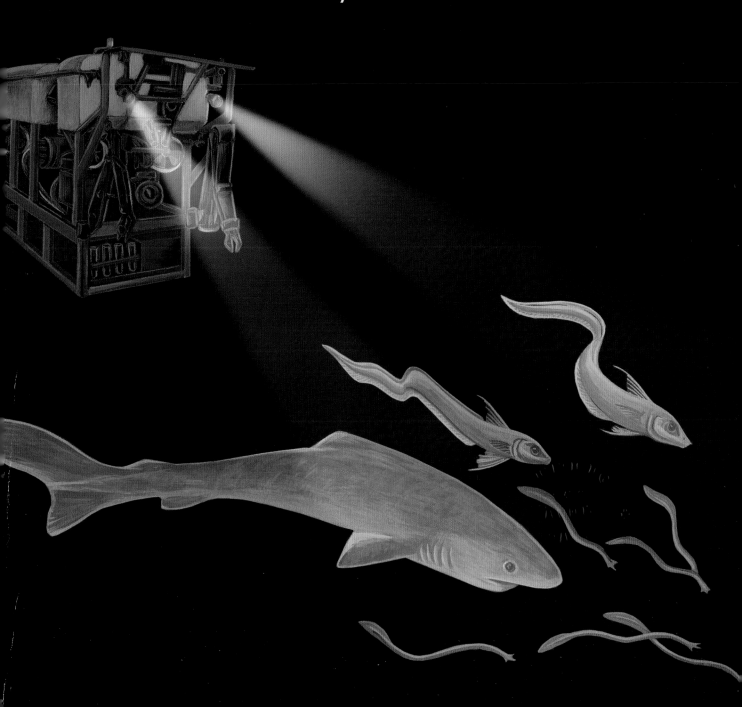

If you dive deep into the ocean,
thousands of feet to the floor,
you would encounter animals
unlike any you have seen before.

As you first dive into the ocean,
the sun is still shining bright.
Brown algae floats near the surface
and makes its own food from the light.

A few of the fronds of *Sargassum*
appear to have two bulging eyes.
A fish with fins like the algae
waits for prey in its natural disguise.

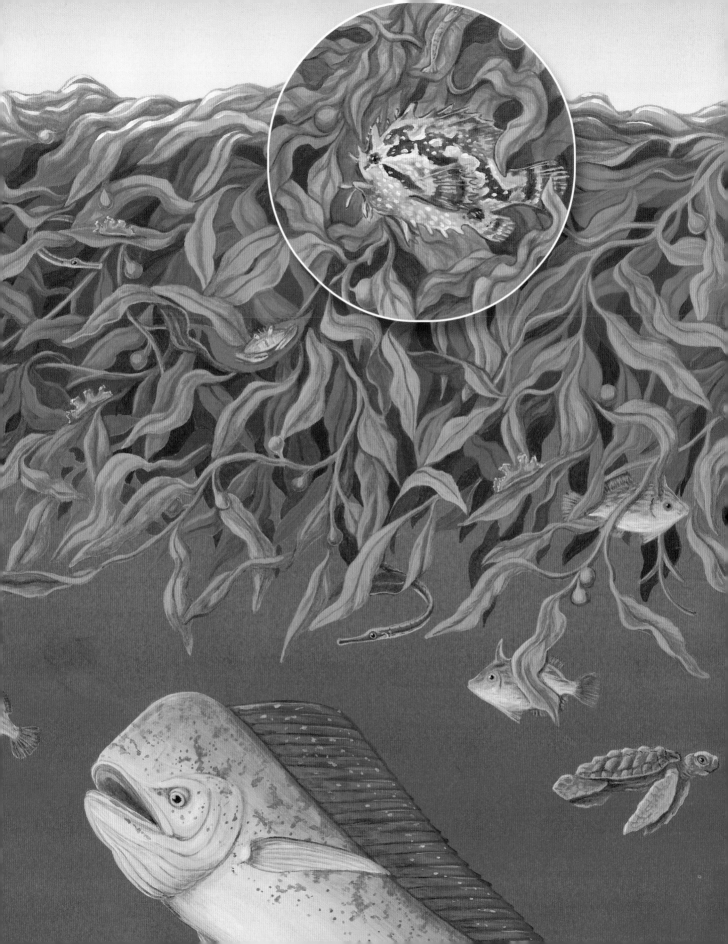

Descending five hundred feet deeper,
you see sharks with bellies that glow
who are schooling in the dimness.
They are small and move rather slow.

Suddenly a marlin approaches,
but that doesn't cause them fright.
One cookiecutter attacks it
and twists off a circular bite.

One thousand feet below sea level,
a fish with protruding jaws
waits patiently in the darkness
with teeth like a raptor's claws.

The viperfish flashes a light,
on a spine attached to its back,
to lure in fish and crustaceans.
One approaches, and it attacks!

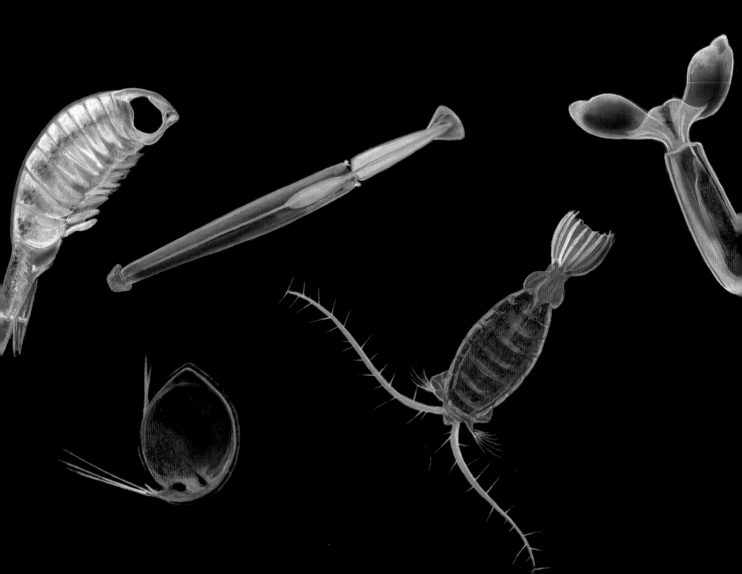

Descending five hundred feet deeper,
you barely see the sunlight
yet millions of tiny plankton
hide in the depths until night.

When the sun goes down in the evening,
they rise to the surface to eat.
The darkness provides them protection
from predators they likely will meet.

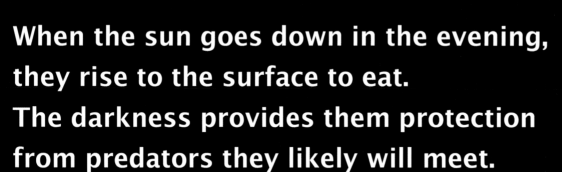

Two thousand feet below sea level,
you notice a beam of blue.
It looks like it shines from a flashlight,
but a fish comes swimming through.

The blue light helps the headlight fish
to see food from far away.
If a shrimp gets caught in the spotlight,
it may become the fish's prey.

Descending five hundred feet deeper,
there in the blackest of darks,
a vampire squid turns inside-out
to hide from an oncoming shark.

The frilled shark investigates closer
by bumping the squid with its nose.
The vampire squid makes its get-away
by spraying out mucus that glows.

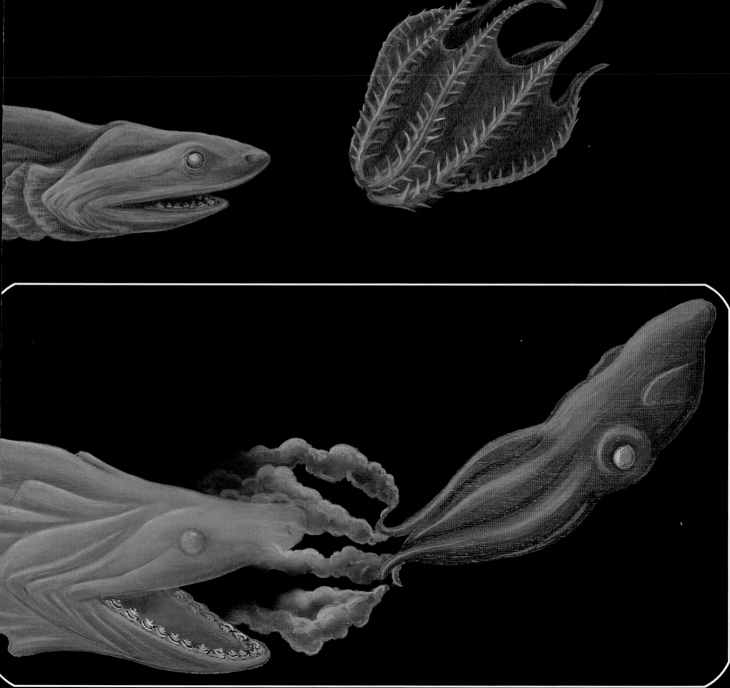

Three thousand feet below sea level,
a fish with binocular sight
keeps staring straight up above it
though there's barely the faintest of light.

The spookfish has long, barrel eyes,
under skin that is totally clear.
The eyes survey the darkness
in hopes that some prey will appear.

Descending five hundred feet deeper,
where algae's unable to grow,
there always appears to be falling
a shower of edible snow.

Marine snow—a mix of bacteria,
dead plankton, and poop by the ton—
allows some animals to feed in
a place that cannot see the sun.

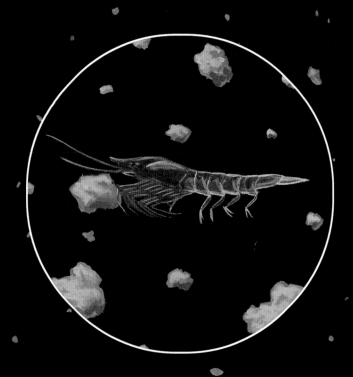

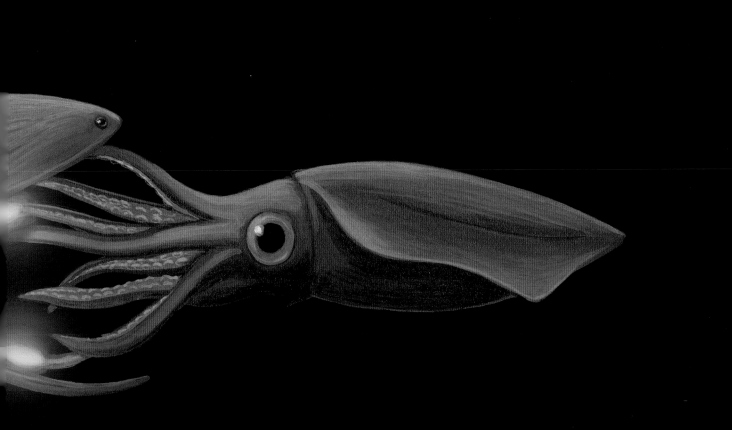

Four thousand feet below sea level,
a fish has been here a week,
waiting for prey it can capture
with a mouth like a pelican's beak.

Pelican eels are not speedy,
nor do they have much strength,
but they can open their big mouths
to swallow prey about their same length.

Descending five hundred feet deeper,
a jelly may soon become prey,
but before the *Atolla* is eaten,
it lights up like a fireworks display.

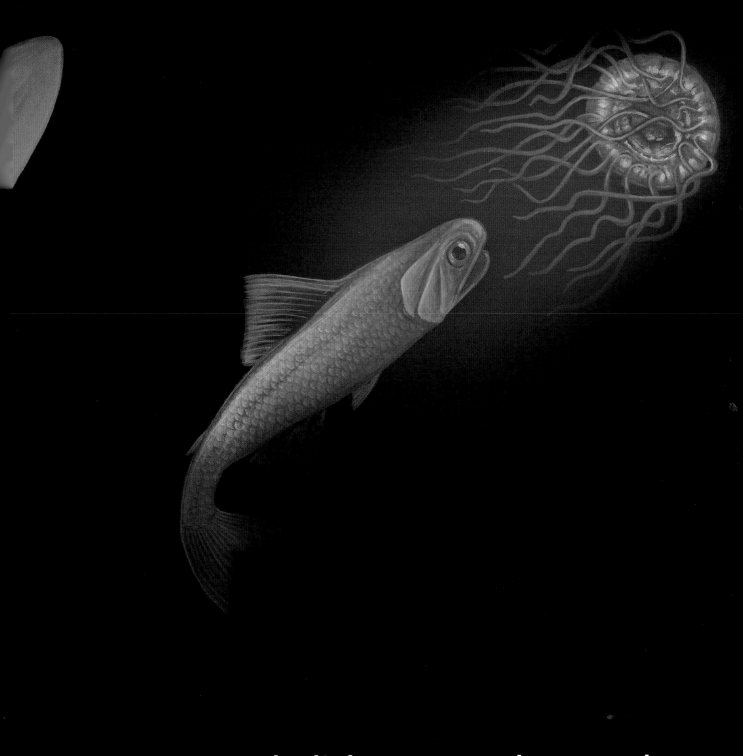

The lights attract a large predator, who responds to the jelly's alarm by eating the smaller predator, saving the *Atolla* from harm.

Five thousand feet below sea level,
a fish who wants to ensure
that prey soon will approach her
uses a light on her head as a lure.

The anglerfish does not hunt alone.
Others are along for the ride:
bacteria that light her fishing lure
and the males attached to her side.

You have reached the ocean floor,
where most animals would not survive.
The temperature is always near freezing.
The pressure would crush them alive.

Yet here at the barren bottom,
an oasis of life appears.
A dead whale sank from the surface.
Some animals will feed here for years.

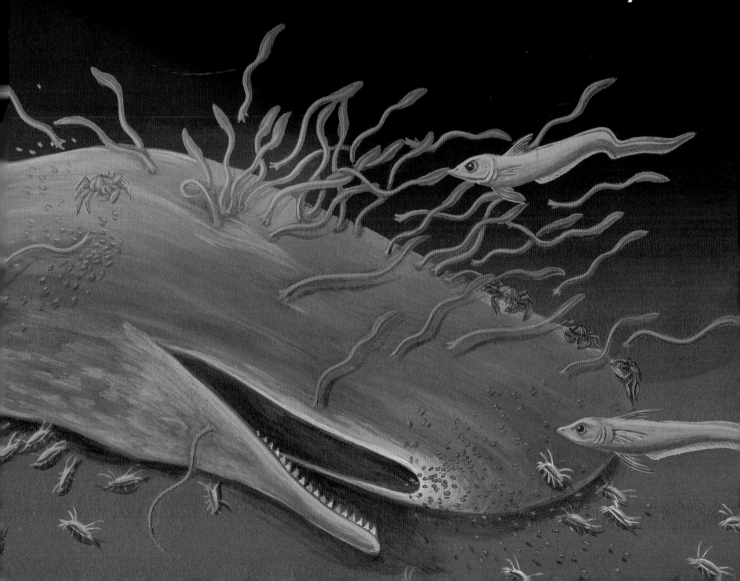

For Creative Minds

Deep Ocean Habitats

Things change the deeper you go in the ocean: light disappears, temperatures grow increasingly colder, and pressure gets much higher. The amount of oxygen in the water decreases with depth but then gets higher again at the bottom! Because these changes affect the types of organisms that can survive there, the ocean is divided into five layers by depth called life zones.

Only the **sunlight zone** receives enough sunlight for algae to convert light into energy (photosynthesis). Because almost all food webs start with plants or algae, this is the zone where the most animals live.

The **twilight zone** still gets some sunlight, but not enough for photosynthesis. The animals that live here either travel to the sunlight zone to feed or depend on food falling from above.

There is no light in the **midnight zone**. Most of the animals that live here produce their own light through bioluminescence.

The **abyssal zone** is pitch black, almost freezing cold, and has little oxygen and incredibly high pressure, yet animals still live here.

In the deep trenches is the **hadal zone**. It is like the abyssal zone, except with even more immense pressure.

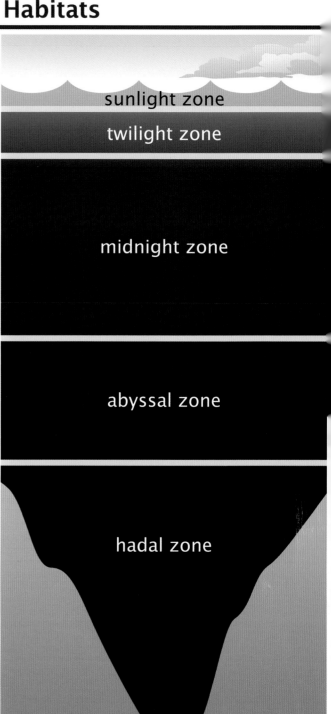

sunlight zone

twilight zone

midnight zone

abyssal zone

hadal zone

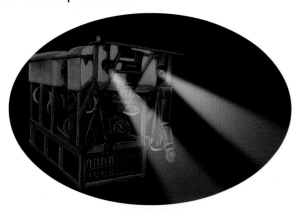

Match the Animal to its Life Zone

If you found these living things at each of these depths, which zone would you be in?

0-660 feet (0-200 meters): sunlight zone
660-3300 feet (200-1,000 meters): twilight zone
3300-13,100 feet (1,000-4,000 meters): midnight zone
13,100-19,700 feet (4,000-6,000 meters): abyssal zone
19,700 feet (6,000 meters) and deeper: hadal zone

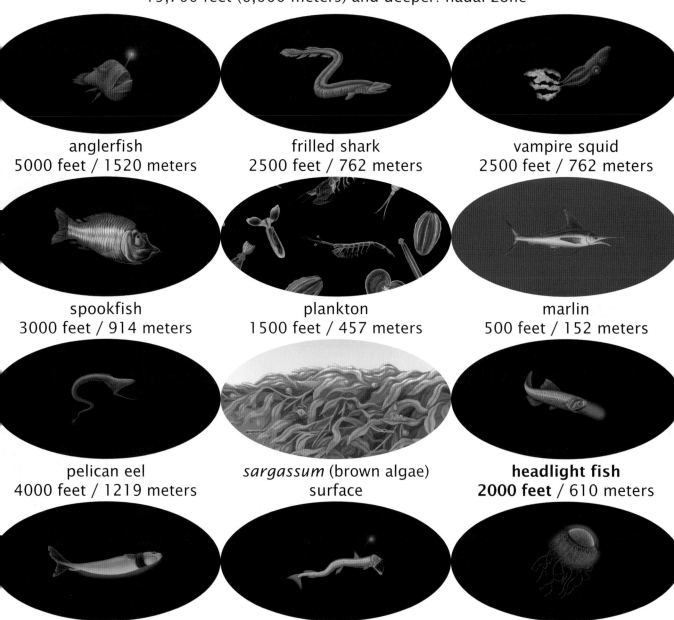

anglerfish 5000 feet / 1520 meters	**frilled shark** 2500 feet / 762 meters	**vampire squid** 2500 feet / 762 meters
spookfish 3000 feet / 914 meters	**plankton** 1500 feet / 457 meters	**marlin** 500 feet / 152 meters
pelican eel 4000 feet / 1219 meters	***sargassum* (brown algae)** surface	**headlight fish** **2000 feet** / 610 meters
cookie cutter shark 500 feet / 152 meters	**viperfish** 1000 feet / 305 meters	***Atolla* jelly** 4500 feet / 1372 meters

Glowing in the Dark

Because sunlight cannot reach deep into water, most of the ocean is pitch black. The deep ocean is so black that if you were down there, you could not even see your own hands or feet. Many animals that live in the dark make their own light—similar to how fireflies light up. The parts of the bodies that make the light are called photophores. When living things make light, it is called bioluminescence.

Deep-sea animals use bioluminescence to lure prey and to find mates. They also can use it to attract, startle and hide from predators. Because the deep ocean is pitch black, you woul not see the animal's body there, but just the lights they make.

Match the deep-sea animals to the descriptions. Answers are upside down, below.

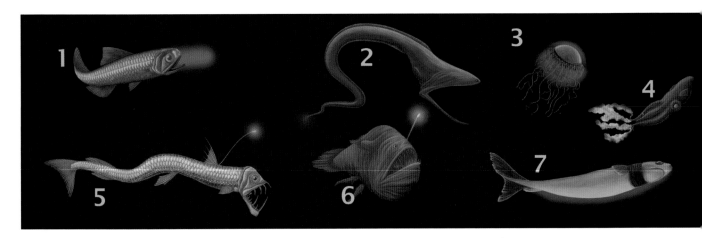

Cookiecutter sharks attract large predators with dark patches on their glowing bellies. The larger animals think they are getting a meal but the cookiecutter sharks bite them instead. Cookiecutters get enough food out of the bites, but the bites don't kill the other animals.

Many animals are attracted to flashing lights. **Viperfish** flash lights along their bellies and at the end of the first long spines just behind their heads. When other animals come to check it out, the viperfish catch their prey.

Vampire squid escape predators by shooting glowing mucus. The predators will see the mucus but not the animal as it swims away.

Just as drivers use car headlights to see at night, **headlight fish** turn on their "headlights" to find prey.

Atolla **jellyfish** light up with blue lights to attract prey. They also light up when threatened by predators, attracting other predators to chase the first ones away.

If you've ever gone fishing, you've probably used a lure to attract the fish. **Anglerfish** do the same thing using light-filled "lures" on top of their heads.

Pelican eels use lures too. Their lures are at the end of their tails and flash pink and red. They pull their tails around close to their mouths so they can grab the animals checking out the lights.

Answers: 1. headlight fish, 2. pelican eel, 3. *Atolla* jellyfish, 4. vampire squid, 5 viperfish, 6. leafvent anglerfish, 7. cookiecutter shark.

Living Under Pressure

queeze your left arm with your right hand. The force you feel from your hand is called ressure. Whenever one thing pushes against another, it creates pressure. As air is ulled towards the earth by gravity, it creates pressure too! At sea level, air creates 14.7 ounds of pressure per square inch. Scientists call these 14.7 pounds per square inch an tmosphere." That's like having a fat cat standing on each square inch of your body!

ater causes even more pressure than air. The deeper you dive into the ocean, e more pressure there is. The pressure you feel increases by one atmosphere very 33 feet farther down you go. The deepest part of the ocean has a ressure of more than 8 tons per square inch. That is too much pressure for umans! But there are still animals that live there, even at that pressure! There e animals living at every depth in the ocean.

One Square Inch

What does pressure feel like in the deep ocean?

Depth below sea level:		PSI (Pounds per Square Inch)	Imagine that this is standing on *every* square inch of your body!
feet	meters		
at sea level	at sea level	14.7 psi	fat cat
500	152.4	223 psi	professional football player
1000	304.8	445 psi	lion
1500	457.2	668 psi	motorcycle
2000	609.6	890 psi	polar bear
2500	762.0	1,114 psi	manatee
3000	914.4	1,335 psi	tiger shark
3500	1066.8	1,558 psi	Holstein cow
4000	1219.2	1,780 psi	smart car and its driver
4500	1371.6	2,003 psi	bison

ndparents, thanks for everything—KK

y of my uncle Marc, who gave me my first camera; and my uncle Keith, who gave me my first microscope—EEH

Thanks to Dr. George I. Matsumoto, Senior Education and Research Specialist at the Monterey Bay Aquarium Research Institute for reviewing the accuracy of the information in this book.

Library of Congress Cataloging-in-Publication Data

Kurtz, Kevin.
  A day in the deep / by Kevin Kurtz ; illustrated by Erin E. Hunter.
     pages cm
  ISBN 978-1-60718-617-5 (English hardcover) -- ISBN 978-1-60718-629-8 (English paperback) -- ISBN 978-1-60718-641-0 (English ebook (downloadable)) -- ISBN 978-1-60718-665-6 (interactive English/Spanish ebook (Web-based)) -- ISBN 978-1-60718-715-8 (Spanish hardcover) -- ISBN 978-1-60718-653-3 (Spanish ebook (downloadable))
  1. Deep-sea animals--Juvenile literature. I. Hunter, Erin E., illustrator. II. Title.
  QL125.5.K87 2013
  591.77--dc23
                          2012045089

Translated into Spanish by Rosalyna Toth: Un día en la profundidad
Lexile® Level: 1050
key phrases for educators: adaptations for survival,
ocean/marine habitat, repeated lines, rhythm or rhyme

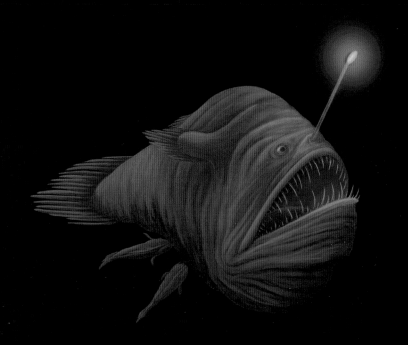

Manufactured in China, June, 2013
This product conforms to CPSIA 2008
First Printing

Sylvan Dell Publishing
Mt. Pleasant, SC 29464
www.SylvanDellPublishing.com